Andrew His Dance

By Andrew Brundidge
& His Mom

Pictures by
Darcy Bell-Myers

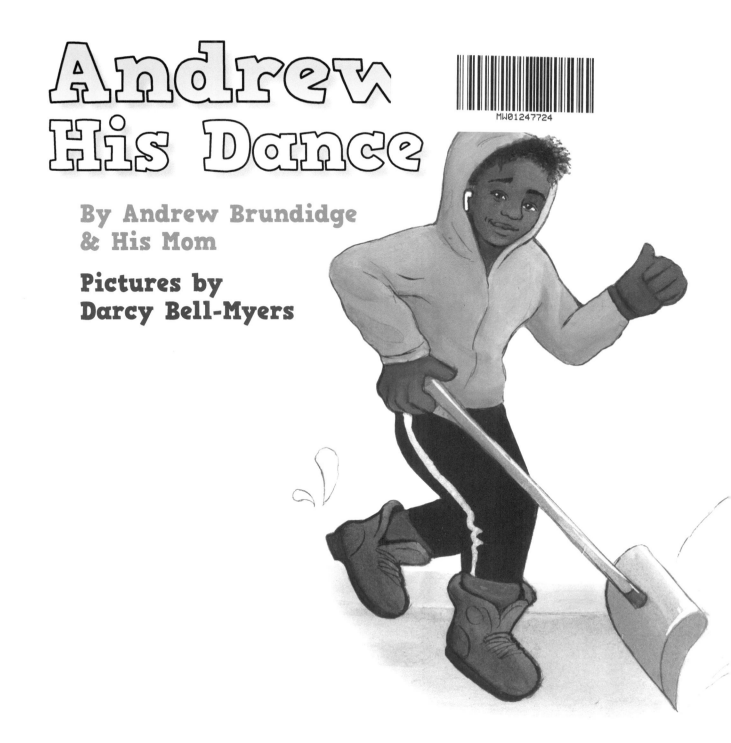

To the late, great Jason Clopton, also known as the Teen Whisperer. You were more than just my therapist. You were my friend and the first person to really see me. Thank you for your love and support. I'll see you again in heaven. — A.B.

Illustrated by Darcy Bell-Myers
ISBN: 978-1-64343-561-9
Library of Congress Control Number: 2024904697
Printed in the United States
First Printing: 2024

28 27 26 25 24   5 4 3 2 1

Cover and interior design by Darcy Bell-Myers

Beaver's Pond Press, Inc.
939 Seventh Street West
St. Paul, MN 55102
(952) 829-8818
www.BeaversPondPress.com

SHElettaMakesMeLaugh.com

Darcy Bell-Myers
Illustration & Design
www.bellmyers.com

I'm Andrew Brundidge. I live in Minnesota with my mom, dad, little brothers, and younger sister. I don't have autism, but my siblings do and they need me!

I spend a lot of time taking care of them.
Or else I'm at school studying,
or working to earn money for college.

That does not leave time for me to do the one thing I love most in this whole world: dancing! So I dance while I'm doing my chores. It makes the time go by faster.

My youngest brother, Daniel, is on the spectrum. He didn't talk for a very long time.

But one day a miracle happened and Daniel started singing. Then his teachers used music to help him speak. Now he talks all the time!

Andrew, I need you to take the trash bins to the curb before you go biking with Suzie and Jawad.

My middle brother, Brandon, has autism too.
He used to be afraid to try new things, like
the boxcar derby race on our street.

But one day Brandon spotted his sign.
It gave him the courage to be brave.
After that, he wasn't scared. Now
he tries new things all the time!

LET'S
GO
BRANDON

My little sister, Cameron, has autism. She used to stay after school to get extra help with her homework.

I didn't think people could see me.
But they do. And you know what?
It feels good.

Tips to Support Children Who Have Autistic Siblings

1. Allow me to have some alone time. Helping my siblings can be exhausting.

2. Ask me about my hobbies and interests. I would like for you to get to know me as an individual.

3. Acknowledge the helpful things I do for my siblings. I want you to see my thoughtfulness.

4. Invite me to hang out or do activities with you. It's okay for me to be away from my siblings.

5. Allow me to plan family activities. This will allow me to feel included.

6. Give me a safe space to share my feelings. Sometimes I am frustrated with my siblings.

7. Remind me that you appreciate the help I give my siblings even when I'm hesitant to do it.

8. Explain autism to me in a way that helps me understand the behaviors of my siblings.

9. Teach me how to respond to people when they stare or ask about my siblings. Role-playing can give me the practice I need.

10. Please show me as much patience and understanding as my siblings even though I am not on the autism spectrum. I need support too.

— LaTonya Land, MEd
School Counselor